Lest We Forget

Grades 4-6

Written by Ruth Solski
Illustrated by Ric Ward

ISBN 0-921511-06-x
Lest We Forget, SSC1-27
Copyright 1989 S&S Learning Materials
Revised July 2003
15 Dairy Avenue
Napanee, Ontario
K7R 1M4
All Rights Reserved * Printed in Canada
A Division of the Solski Group

Published in Canada by:
S&S Learning Materials
15 Dairy Avenue
Napanee, Ontario
K7R 1M4
www.sslearning.com

© S&S Learning Materials

Look for Other Seasonal Resources

Published by:
S&S Learning Materials
15 Dairy Avenue
Napanee, Ontario
K74 1M4

Remembrance Day

Table of Contents

 # Remembrance Day

Expectations

The information and activities about Remembrance Day are designed to help students achieve the following:

- to recognize the sacrifice made by thousands of Canadians in the First and Second World Wars and the Korean War

- to develop an understanding of the significance of Remembrance Day

- to develop an awareness of the ceremonies and rites of the past as they are reflected in the present

- to appreciate the realities and complexities of war

- to appreciate the qualities of endurance and courage and of devotion to the principles of freedom within our multicultural society

- to learn to resolve conflict successfully

- to celebrate peace

List of Vocabulary

Remembrance Day Words

November, World War I, World War II, Korean War, troops, soldiers, infantrymen, pilots, sailors, monument, cenotaph, poppy, Royal Canadian Legion, Peace Tower, The National War Memorial, Flanders Fields, crosses, wreath, veterans, march, parades, bands, choirs, Two-Minute Silence, bugle, Last Post, Reveille, D-Day, army, airforce, marines, navy, Red Cross, memory, remember, praise, dead, laud, honour, fought, war, deed, cemetery, hero, heroism, heroic, pride, devotion, virile, gallant, valiant, aloof, sacrifice, tyranny, oppression, freedom, dignity, homage, courage, devotion, duty, tribute, dedicate, brave, bravery, victory, victors, allies, defeat, proud, surrender, loyalty, valour, respect

Famous Countries and Cities

Normandy, Pearl Harbor, Nagasaki, Dunkirk, England, London, France, Paris, Belgium, Holland, Germany, Berlin, Hiroshima, Tokyo, Japan, Moscow, Russia (Soviet Union), Poland, Warsaw

Famous War Leaders

Adolph Hitler, Winston Churchill, Benito Mussolini, Franklin D. Roosevelt, Hideki Tojo

Military Equipment

tanks, airplanes, jeeps, warships, aircraft, aircraft carriers, artillery, guns, bayonet, helmet, uniform, atomic bomb, bombs, grenade, buzz bombs, arms, shells, gas masks, radar, submarines, machine gun, torpedoes

Remembrance Day

Other War Words

air raid siren, prisoner of war, prison camps, concentration camps, trenches, "kamikazi", "blitzkrieg", "blitz", battle, front, fight, kill, wound, destroy, shoot, bomb, spy, defend, battlefield

List of Resources

1. Herbert Walther ed. <u>Adolph Hitler</u>. Bison Books
2. Chaz Bowyer. <u>Supermarine Spitfire</u>. Arms & Armour Press
3. H.P. Willmott. <u>B-17 Flying Fortress</u>. Arms & Armour Press
4. Tim Healy. <u>Secret Armies</u>. MacDonald & Co.
5. Correlli Barnett. <u>The Great War</u>. Peerage Books, London
6. G.C. Skipper. <u>World at War - D. Day</u>. Children's Press, Chicago
7. R. Conrad Stein. <u>World at War - Hiroshima</u>. Children's Press, Chicago
8. R. Conrad Stein. <u>World at War - Dunkirk</u>. Children's Press, Chicago
9. Lt.-Col. A.J. Barker. <u>Struka Ju-87</u>. Arms and Armour Press Ltd.
10. William Newly Grant. <u>P-51 Mustang</u>. Arms and Armour Press Ltd.
11. Christopher Shores. <u>Air Aces</u>. Bison Books
12. Brian Williams. <u>The Great Book of Battles</u>. Ray Rourke Pub. Co. Inc.
13. Gene Gurney. <u>Flying Aces of World War I</u>. Scholastic Book Services
14. Matthew Holden. <u>War in the Trenches</u>. Wayland Publishers Ltd.
15. Dorothy Hoobler. <u>An Album of World War I</u>. Franklin Watts
16. Christopher Maynard & David Jefferis. <u>The Aces: Pilots and Planes of World War I</u>. Watts
17. Russell Potter Reeder. <u>Bold Leaders of World War I</u>. Little Publishers

Teacher Input Suggestions

Length of Time:

This theme may be used during the entire month of November. It does not have to dwell on the ugly aspects of just war but on peace, friendship, respect, honour, the brotherhood of man, solving problems, getting along, etc.

Planning Ahead:

Look for the following items prior to the theme.

Pictures and Photographs of the Peace Tower, The National Memorial Monument, the real poppy, war scenes, military personnel, cenotaphs, monuments, memorials, military equipment, Flanders Fields, war heroes, peace symbols

Remembrance Day

Films, filmstrips and videos that pertain to World War I, World War II, and the Korean War.

Books that show the three wars, military equipment, countries where the wars were located, war leaders, war heroes, etc.

Discussion Topics:

The selection of topics and the depth in which they are discussed is left to the discretion of the teacher.

- What is a War? - causes
- World War One - causes, countries involved, results of the war, Canada's involvement
- World War Two - causes, countries involved, results of the war, Canada's involvement
- Korean War - causes, countries involved, results of the war, Canada's involvement
- Famous War Leaders from World War I and World War II - Winston Churchill, Adolph Hitler, Benito Mussolini, Hideki Tojo, Franklin D. Roosevelt
- Peace - Peace Keeping Organizations, The United Nations, The Noble Peace Prize, Lester B. Pearson, Canadian Peace Keeping Operations, The International Law of Peace
- Freedom and Its Importance; countries that do not have the same freedoms as Canada Examples: Cuba, Russia, Korea
- Symbols of Peace - dove, white flag, olive branch, The Tree of the Great Peace 1390, Calumet or Peace Pipe, peace offering, Peace International Bridge, The International Peace Gardens
- Friendship - importance, treatment
- Respect - how to show respect, why it is important
- Heroism and Heroic Deeds - brainstorm heroic acts, the attributes of a hero
- Memories - brainstorm for important memories, discuss war memories and their effects on people

Literature Ideas:

1. Choose a selection of novels the students may read during the month of November that pertain to families that lived during a wartime era. Select one of the novels to read to the class and to discuss. The novels could be read independently or as a large group reading assignment.

    Examples of Books:
    - Sadako and the 1000 Paper Cranes by Eleanor Coerr
    - Number the Stars by Lois Lowry
    - Sky is Falling by Kit Pearson
    - Mystery at Black Rock Island by Robert Sutherland
    - Rilla of Ingleside by Lucy Maud Montgomery
    - Summer of My German Soldier by Bette Green
    - Snow Treasure by Marie McSwigan

2. Read poetry about heroic deeds, Remembrance Day, battles, war, life during the war, etc. The following are examples of poems that you might find useful in helping your students gain a better appreciation of the meaning of Remembrance Day.

Remembrance Day

- "War" by Langston Hughes
- "And Death Shall Have No Dominion" by Dylan Thomas
- "To an Athlete Dying Young" by A.E. Housman
- "For an Old Man" by Floris Clark
- "In Flanders Fields" by John McCrae
- "The Man He Killed" by Thomas Hardy
- "Anthem for Doomed Youth" by Wilfred Owens
- "Arms and the Boy" by Wilfred Owens
- "For the Fallen" by Laurence Binyon
- "The Conquerors" by Phyllis McGinley
- "Range Finding" by Robert Frost
- "Music 1939 - 40" by John Masefield
- "An Irish Airman Foresees His Death" by William Butler Yeats
- "The Dying Eagle" by E. J. Pratt
- "My Brother" by Mona Gould
- "Suicide in the Trenches" by Siegfried Sassoon
- "Prayer for Victory" by Dick Diespecker
- "The Dead" by Ruperte Brooke
- "Heroes We Never Name" by Lucille Ford
- "Veterans Day" by Kate Clark
- "Armistice Day Vision" by Alice Hoffman

The following poem could be used as an introduction to this unit or it could be presented as a choral speaking piece during a Remembrance Day Ceremony at school.

Why Wear A Poppy?

"Please wear a poppy", the lady said.
And held one forth, but I shook my head.
Then I stopped and watched as she offered them there,
And her face was old and lined with care.
But beneath the scars the years had made
There remained a smile that refused to fade.

A boy came whistling down the street,
Bouncing along on care-free feet.
His smile was full of joy and fun.
"Lady'", said he, "may I have one?"
When she pinned it on he turned to say,
"Why do I wear a poppy today?"

The lady smiled in her wistful way,
And answered, "This is Remembrance Day."
And the poppy there is the symbol for
The gallant men who died in war.
And because they did, you and I are free
That's why we wear a poppy, you see

I had a boy about your size
With golden hair and big blue eyes.
He loved to play and jump and shout,
Free as a bird he would race about.
As the years went by he learned and grew,
And became a man --- as you will too.

He was fine and strong, with a boyish smile
But he'd seemed with us such a little while
When war broke out and he went away,
I still remember his face that day,
When he smiled at me and said, "good-bye"
"I'll be back soon, Mom, please don't cry."

"But the war went on and he had to stay,
And all I could do is wait and pray.
His letters told of his terrible fight,
(I can see it still in my dreams at night.)
With the tanks and guns and cruel barbed wire.
And the mines and bullets, the bombs and fire."

"Till at last, at last, the war was won ---
And that's why we wear a poppy, son."
The small boy turned as if to go,
Then said, "Thanks, lady, I'm glad to know.
That sure did sound like an awful fight,
But your son --- did he come back all right?"

A tear rolled down each faded cheek;
She shook her head, but didn't speak.
I slunk away in a sort of shame,
And if you were me you'd have done the same;
For thanks in giving, is oft delayed,
Though our freedom was bought --- and thousands paid!

And so when we see a poppy worn,
Let us reflect on the burden borne
By those who gave their very all!
When asked to answer their country's call
That we at home in peace might live.
Then wear a poppy! Remember and give.

Music:

Teach songs about peace, Remembrance Day, friendship and freedom. **Examples**: It Takes Time, Bridge Over Troubled Water, Blowin' in the Wind, Born Free. It may also be fun for the students to learn songs sung during the war years.

Set up a listening centre so students can listen to the music that was popular during the wartime eras.

Perhaps the students may like to learn some of the dances enjoyed in that time period.

 # Remembrance Day

Art:

Involve your students in a poster contest. Some of the themes may be about friendship, peace, freedom, war, or Remembrance Day.

Wreaths could be made to hang on the classroom door or at home on the front door.

Drama:

Your students may like to organize a simple Remembrance Day Service for the school or the classroom. Encourage them to incorporate poetry, music and stories in their service.

The poem entitled "Why Wear a Poppy?" could be used as a choral speaking exercise.

Guests:

Invite a war veteran or a member of your local Canadian Legion to speak to the class about Remembrance Day and to answer students' questions. You may also wish to involve someone who is presently in the armed services to speak about how the Canadian military act as peace keepers in different parts of the world.

Displays:

Display books on Remembrance Day, the wars, war equipment and famous leaders around the room.

Encourage your students to bring in memorabilia that their grandparents or their great grandparents collected during the war years such as medals, uniforms, black and white photographs. Display the items on a "Memories" table.

Mapping:

Obtain a large map of the world. Lay the map on a large table. Using modelling clay and a popsicle stick, make flags of the different countries involved in the war. Have the students research to find out which countries were the Allies and which countries belonged to the Axis during World War II. Assign a country to each student. The student will have to research the flag and illustrate it. The flag will then be affixed to the popsicle stick that is embedded into the modelling clay. The student will then locate the country on the map and place the flag on it.

Free Materials

All the following materials are available free to school libraries. Make your requests on school letterhead. The teacher-librarian should request the materials.

Write to: Communications Division
                 Veterans Affairs Canada
                 Room 1525A, 66 Slater Street
                 Ottawa, Ontario
                 K1A 0P4
or visit the Veteran's Affairs website at www.vac-acc.gc.ca

- **A Day of Remembrance** - Available in class sets (bilingual); Includes - Why remember? Who do we remember?; What should we remember?; How do we remember?; Well illustrated with black and white photographs

- **Canada in the First World War and the Road to Vimy Ridge** - bilingual

- **Lieutenant Colonel John McCrae** - short, bilingual booklet on the author of "In Flanders Fields"; photograph of his grave; copy of his poem; history of the poppy as a symbol

- **Valour Remembered: Canada & The Second World War** - bilingual; chapters on how the war began, Battle of the Atlantic, defence of Hong Kong, raid on Dieppe, conquest of Sicily, war at sea and in the air, liberation of the Netherlands, etc.; well illustrated with black and white photographs

- **Valour Remembered: Canada & The First World War** - similar to above with maps, chapters on the various battles at Vimy, The Somme, Passchendale, Hill 70, etc.

- **Valour Remembered: Canadians in Korea** - bilingual; includes maps, chapters on the background of the conflict; Canadian troops in action; various battles

- **Valour at Sea: Canada's Merchant Navy** - bilingual

- **Native Soldiers, Foreign Battlefields** - bilingual

There are also numerous posters on war themes.

Distributors:

The following list contains addresses of distributors from whom you may wish to order films, slides and other materials. There may be a small charge. Check before ordering.

- Canadian War Museum, 330 Sussex Drive, Ottawa, Ontario, K1A 0M8
  Attention: Curator of War Art; Telephone: (613) 992-4330

- Modern Talking Pictures Service, Inc., 143 Sparks Avenue, Willowdale, Ontario;
  Telephone: (416) 369-4094

- Ontario Educational Communications Authority (OECA), Canada Square, 2180 Yonge Street, Toronto, Ontario, M4S 2C1; Telephone: (416) 484-2700

- Ontario Provincial Command, Royal Canadian Legion, 218 Richmond Street West, Toronto, Ontario, M5V 1V8; Telephone: (416) 598-4466

- UNICEF Ontario, 101-38 Berwick Avenue, Toronto, Ontario, M5P 1H1; Telephone: (416) 487-4153

- United National Association in Canada, 808-63 Sparks Avenue, Ottawa, Ontario, K1P 5A6;
  Telephone: (613) 232-5751

Student Evaluation Sheet

Topic : _____

Date : _____

Evaluation Marks:
S - Satisfactory
I - Improving
N - Needs Improvement
U - Unsatisfactory

Students' Names

Remembrance Day

Student Activity Record

Name: _____   Date: _____

Colour each circle red when your activity has been completed and marked.

Reading:

1. What is War? ○
2. World War I ○
3. Fighting Conditions During World War I ○
4. Consequences of World War I ○
5. World War II ○
6. Consequences of World War II ○
7. The National War Memorial ○
8. The Remembrance Day Service ○
9. The Two-Minute Silence ○
10. The Flowers of Remembrance ○
11. The Peace Tower ○
12. Famous Canadian War Heroes ○
13. John McCrae ○

Brainstorming:

1. If you could wish upon a star.. ○
2. Remembrance Day is..... ○
3. War Alert! ○
4. A Remembrance Day Poster ○
5. Fighting at the Front ○
6. Acts of Courage ○
7. Planning an Interview ○
8. Ruled by a Dictator ○
9. An Honour Role ○

Research:

1. War leaders ○
2. The Flower of Remembrance ○
3. Important Places ○

4. Researching a Country ○
5. Canadian Medals ○
6. War Machines ○
7. The Atomic Bomb ○
8. Fun With Maps ○

Word Study:

1. Lest We Forget Crossword ○
2. Remembrance Day Word Search ○
3. Syllabication ○
4. Matching Antonyms ○
5. Matching Synonyms ○
6. Writing the Plural Form ○
7. Working with Parts of Speech ○
8. Spelling Riddles ○
9. Anagrams ○

Creative Writing:

1. Poetry Search ○
2. A Sentence of Remembrance ○
3. Sentences of Thanksgiving ○
4. Remembrance Day Thoughts ○
5. Story Writing ○
6. A Remembrance Day Card ○
7. Writing a Stair Poem ○
8. A Cinquain of Remembrance ○
9. Remembrance Day Haiku ○
10. Acrostic Poetry ○

Remembrance Day

Information Card 1

What is War?

War is a struggle that takes place when two large groups try to conquer or destroy each other. Since the beginning of time, there have been many kinds of wars. In early times families fought against families, tribes fought against tribes and followers of one religion fought against followers of another. During modern times, wars have been fought between nations or groups of nations.

For hundreds of years, wars have been going on somewhere in the world nearly all the time. People hate wars because they always cause great hardship and suffering. In modern times, most nations or groups try to settle problems peacefully. Sometimes war results from a disagreement between nations and sometimes from a desire for conquest.

In ancient times, people often fought so that they could get enough to eat. They would make war on neighbours in order to obtain new lands to grow food. During the 1600s through to the 1800s, this kind of war took place in North America between the pioneers and the Native People. The Native People wanted to roam freely over the land, hunting, trapping or fishing whereas the pioneers wanted to clear the land to plant their crops. Frequent wars and battles took place during this time period.

The people of ancient empires fought wars for wealth. The ruler of an empire and his or her advisors made the decision to conquer new lands for the purpose of collecting taxes from the people. They would hire armies to do their fighting. The people were not driven from their lands.

Alexander the Great led his soldiers against the Persian Empire in 334 B.C. The common people of the invaded lands paid little attention to the invasion. They only hoped their property would not be destroyed. They did not care which ruler collected the taxes.

Sometimes wars were fought by European nations to gain or increase their power. These wars united the people and strengthened the government.

Often countries feared the possibility of an attack and maintain armed forces to defend themselves. A country might fear a particular country and might choose its own time to strike the first blow. It might also choose to conquer some weaker neighbour to increase its own resources as a defense against attack.

There are usually various reasons and causes for a nation to make war against another nation. There are differences between the causes and reasons of a war. The government always states the "reasons" for the war in order to unite the people in the war effort. The "causes" of a war may be selfish, base, or even wicked while the reasons are usually lofty and noble.

Remembrance Day

Reading Activity 1

Read the Information Card One entitled *"What is War?"*

Complete the following activities.

1. Wars have been taking place since the beginning of time. Record **five** reasons why wars occur.

   _____
   _____
   _____
   _____
   _____
   _____
   _____
   _____

2. What are the diffences between the "*causes*" and "*reasons*" of a war?

   _____
   _____
   _____
   _____
   _____
   _____
   _____

3. Why do people hate wars?

   _____
   _____

4. Write a paragraph stating your feelings about war.

   _____
   _____
   _____
   _____
   _____
   _____
   _____

Remembrance Day

Information Card 2

World War I

World War I was originally called "The Great War" and it began in 1914 and ended in 1918. The assassination of Archduke Francis Ferdinand of Austria-Hungary in Sarajevo, the capital of Austria-Hungary's province of Bosnia-Herzegovina, sparked the outbreak of World War I. This was not the chief cause as many other factors had been developing in various countries during the 1800s. The main causes of World War I were the rise of nationalism, the build-up of military might, competition for colonies and a system of military alliances.

World War I began in the states of the Balkan Peninsula, the site of many small wars. This area in Europe has often been called "the powder keg of Europe". In the early 1900s, the Balkan States fought the Ottoman Empire in the First Balkan War (1912 -1913) and again in the Second Balkan War (1913). The major powers stayed out of the first two Balkan Wars but they could not escape involvement during the third Balkan crisis.

Archduke Francis Ferdinand, heir to the throne of Austria-Hungary decided to tour Bosnia-Herzegovina, with his wife Sophie, to ease tensions between the Balkans and Austria-Hungary. As the couple rode through Sarajevo on June 28, 1914, an assassin jumped onto their automobile and fired two shots. The Archduke and his wife died almost instantly. The assassin, Gavrilo Princip, was linked to a Serbian terrorist group called the "Black Hand".

This assassination gave Austria-Hungary an excuse to crush Serbia, its long time enemy in the Balkans.

Important dates that took place during World War I are listed below. The events with asteriks (*) pertain to important Canadian events that took place during the time of The Great War.

Important Dates to Remember

Year - 1914

June 28 - Archduke Francis Ferdinand of Austria-Hungary was assassinated by Gavrilo Princip in Sarajevo.

July 28 - Austria-Hungary declared war on Serbia.

August 4 - Germany invaded Belgium, a neutral country, and started the fighting.

      * Britain declares war on Germany; Canada is automatically at war.

August 10 - Austria-Hungary invaded Russia, opening the fighting on the Eastern Front

Remembrance Day

Information Card 2

Important Dates to Remember Cont'd

September 8-9 - The Allies stopped the Germans in France in the First Battle of the Marne.

October - * 32 100 Canadian troops sailed to England, where the First Canadian Division is found.

Year - 1915

February 18 - Germany began to blockade Great Britain.

April 25 - Allied troops landed on the Gallipoli Peninsula.

* Second Battle of Ypres: Canadian troops hold the line in the face of the first gas attack of the war.

May 23 - Italy declared war on Austria-Hungary and an Italian Front soon developed.

September - * First and Second Canadian Divisions are united to form the Canadian Corps.

Year - 1916

February 21 - The Germans opened the Battle of Verdun.

May 31 - June 1 - The British fleet fought the German fleet in the Battle of Jutland.

* Lieutenant-General Julian Byng becomes commander of the Canadian Corps.

June - * Battle of Mount Sorrel

July 1 - The Allies launched the Battle of the Somme.

September - November - * Canadians involved in the Battle of the Somme.

Year - 1917

February 1 - Germany resumed unrestricted submarine warfare.

* Prime Minister Borden attends the first Imperial War Conference in London, England.

Remembrance Day

Information Card 2

Important Dates to Remember Cont'd

April 6 - The United States declared war on Germany.

 * Battle of Vimy Ridge, the most famous Canadian battle of the war.

June 24 - American troops began landing in France.

 * Billy Bishop was awarded the Victoria Cross.

 * Arthur Currie becomes commander of the Canadian Corp.

August - * Military Service (conscription)

November - * Battle of Passchendael

December 6 - * The Halifax Explosion

December 15 - Russia signed an armistice with Germany, ending the fighting on the Eastern Front.

Year - 1918

January 18 - President Woodrow Wilson announced his Fourteen Points as the basis for peace.

March 3 - Russia signed the Treaty of Brest-Litovsk.

 *Anti-conscription riots in Québec City

March 21 - Germany launched the first of its final three offences on the Western Front.

April - * Roy Brown was credited with shooting down the "Red Baron" von Richthofen.

May - * Women's Franchise Act gives the vote to women in federal elections in Canada.

August to November

 *The Canadian Corps leads the Allied armies into the final offensive of the war.

November 11 - * Armistice with Germany ends World War I

Remembrance Day

Reading Activity Card 2

Read the Information Card entitled *"World War I"*.

Answer the following questions with complete sentence answers.

1. What event sparked the beginning of World War I?
   _____
   _____

2. a) Why do you think the Balkan Peninsula was described as "the powder keg of Europe"?
      _____
      _____

   b) How do you know that this area of Europe is still a "powder keg"?
      _____
      _____

3. On August 4, 1914, Britain declared war on Germany. Why was Canada automatcially involved in the war?
   _____
   _____

4. How many Canadian troops were sent to England?
   _____

5. What type of warfare was used at the Second Battle of Ypres?
   _____

6. Which battle was the most important for Canadian troops?
   _____

7. Which Canadian was awarded the Victoria Cross?
   _____

8. What does the word "conscription" mean?
   _____
   _____

9. Which province in Canada was unhappy with the conscription law?
   _____

Remembrance Day

Information Card 3

Fighting Conditions During World War I

Before the Great War began, many countries were building strong armies and navies. Countries such as Germany and England were competing for seapower by building heavily armed modern battleships. Advances in technology and the techniques of industrialization increased the destructive power of military forces. Machine guns and other new arms that could fire more accurately and more rapidly were produced. Troops and supplies could move faster from place to place by steamships and railroads.

World War I was fought on land, in the air, and on the water. The airplane was first used in combat during World War I. These bombers held a pilot and a gunner and carried bombs under their wings. The tank was invented by the British. Tanks could rip through barbed wire and cross trenches. They held crews inside who gunned down enemies. The machine gun's rapid fire slaughtered many attacking infantrymen. It made World War I more deadly than earlier wars. The submarine was a warship that could fight under the water. It fired torpedoes that struck surface ships, and caused them to explode.

Trench warfare took place during World War I. A system of trenches were dug by the opposing sides between France, Belgium and Germany. This was called the "Western Front". A "front-line" trench was 1.8 metres to 2.4 metres deep and wide enough for two men to pass one another. Dugouts in the sides of the trenches protected the men during enemy fire. Barbed wire helped protect the front-line trenches from surprise attacks. Support trenches with field artillery were set up behind the front-line trenches.

Between the enemy lines lay a stretch of ground called "no man's land". This area could be from 2.7 metres wide at some points to more than 1.6 kilometres wide at others. Artillery fire tore up this area making it difficult to cross during an attack.

A soldier's life in the trenches was miserable and often very wet and uncomfortable. The smell of dead bodies hung in the air and rats caused constant problems. Time in the trenches would be filled with dull routines except during an attack. Soldiers took turns standing guard, repairing the trenches, kept phone wires in working order, brought food from behind the battle lines and at night repaired barbed wire and tried to find out information about the enemy.

Remembrance Day

Fighting Conditions During World War I Cont'd

The soldiers were pinned in the trenches by enemy artillery and machine guns. The Allies kept trying to break through the German lines. They would have the artillery bombard the enemy front-line trenches. The infantry than attacked as the commanders shouted "Over the top!". The soldiers scrambled quickly out of the trenches and began to run across "no man's land" with fixed bayonets. Grenades were thrown at the enemy trenches and the soldiers struggled to get through the barb wire. Unfortunately the artillery failed to wipe out all resistance and enemy machine guns slaughtered wave after wave of advancing infantry.

The Allies and the Germans had developed new weapons which they hoped would help to break through these strong lines of defense. In April 1915, the Germans first released a poisonous gas over the Allied lines in the Second Battle of Ypres. The fumes from the gas caused vomiting and suffocation.

The Allies used a poisonous gas as well and gas masks became a necessary piece of equipment in the trenches. The flame thrower was another new weapon which shot out a stream of burning fuel.

Remembrance Day

Reading Activity 3

Read the Information Card entitled *"Fighting Conditions During World War I"*.

Complete each sentence with words from the Information Card.

1. _____ and _____ were building heavily armed modern _____ because they were competing for _____.

2. _____ were invented by the British and they could rip through _____ wire and cross _____.

3. The _____ _____ rapid fire _____ many attacking infantrymen.

4. During World War I _____ fought from _____ dug into the ground.

5. Between the trenches was an area called _____ which was very _____ to cross.

6. Life in the trenches was _____, very _____ and _____.

7. The soldiers were pinned in the trenches by enemy _____ and _____ _____.

8. Poisonous _____ released by the Germans caused _____ and _____.

9. Many men were slaughtered by _____ machine guns when they tried to get through the barbed wire.

10. The _____ was used for the first time in _____ during World War I.

11. _____ and _____ provided countries with a greater _____ power than ever before.

12. A system of trenches were dug between _____, _____ and _____.

Remembrance Day

Information Card 4

Consequences of World War I

World War I left great destruction and many casualties. Nearly ten million soldiers died as a result of the war and about 21 million were wounded. The new weapons developed during this era, especially the machine gun, slaughtered many men. Germany, Russia, and France lost the most servicemen.

Many important buildings, churches, and homes were destroyed during the war. France and Belgium were hit the hardest. Armies destroyed farms and villages as they passed through them or dug trenches to fight battles. Factories, bridges, and railroad tracks were wrecked by bombs and artillery shells.

Wars cost countries millions of dollars which they often had to borrow from wealthy countries. When the war was over, the countries were left in debt and it took a long time to pay the money back. Money was also needed to rebuild the country to its former state. Soldiers returning home did not have work as factories and businesses had been destroyed. Countries in which the war had been fought were left with heavy war debts, poor economies, and no markets to ship their exports.

World War I changed the political climate in some of the countries. Four monarchies toppled after the war. Czar Nicholas II of Russia was the first monarch to lose his power in 1917. Kaiser Wilhelm II of Germany and Emperor Charles of Austria-Hungary left their thrones in 1918. The Ottoman Sultan, Mohammed VI, lost his throne in 1922.

New countries were formed. The pre-war territory of Austria-Hungary formed the independent republics of Austria, Hungary and Czechoslovakia as well as parts of Italy, Poland, Romania, and Yugoslavia. Russia and Germany gave up territory to Poland. Finland and the Baltic States of Estonia, Latvia, and Lithuania gained their independence from Russia. World War I gave the Communists an opportunity to seize power in Russia.

World War I brought enormous changes to society in many of the countries. France lost many more young men than any of the other countries, and its population dropped during the 1920s because of a low birth rate. Millions of people were uprooted during the war, and lost everything they owned. Those who returned found their homes, villages, and farms in ruins. Many people chose to make a living in urban areas instead of returning to their farms. Women found their independence during the war; they held down many jobs that men had left to fight the war. They did not want to give up their new-found independence. Many countries had granted women the right to vote in elections after the war. European attitudes and ideals had been shattered, and they lost confidence and optimism in their way of life and culture.

Remembrance Day

Reading Activity 4

Read the Information Card entitled *"Consequences of World War I"*.

Locate the sentence on the Information Card that proves each statement below is correct. Write the first **five** words of the sentence on the line and the paragraph number.

1. War destroys buildings and residences.

   _____ Paragraph # _____

2. Travelling in war-torn countries was difficult after the war.

   _____ Paragraph # _____

3. Many soldiers died or were wounded during World War I.

   _____ Paragraph # _____

4. People lost their homes and all their possessions during the war.

   _____ Paragraph # _____

5. Wars are very expensive and leave countries in poor situations.

   _____ Paragraph # _____

6. Some leaders lost their positions and power after the war.

   _____ Paragraph # _____

7. Countries had to give back territory they had taken.

   _____ Paragraph # _____

8. Farmers did not return to the land but settled in cities instead after the war.

   _____ Paragraph # _____

9. Women enjoyed the new independence given to them during the war.

   _____ Paragraph # _____

10. Europeans no longer felt good about their way of life and culture.

   _____ Paragraph # _____

11. Some countries regained their independence after the war.

   _____ Paragraph # _____

12. There was very little work for the soldiers when they returned home at the end of the war.

   _____ Paragraph # _____

Remembrance Day

Information Card 5

World War II: 1939 - 1945

World War II involved 59 nations by the end of the war. It killed more people, destroyed more property, disrupted more lives, and had more far-reaching consequences than any other war in history. Historians feel that the unsolved problems felt by World War I and the treaties that ended it, created new political and economic problems.

Forceful dictators in Germany, Italy and Japan took advantage of these problems. They wanted to conquer additional territory to support their growing populations. After World War I, treaties created hostile feelings leaving countries such as Italy and Japan dissatisfied vowing to take action on their own. Countries such as Germany, Austria, Hungary, Bulgaria and Turkey were very unhappy as the treaties stripped them of territory and arms. They also had to make "reparations" (payments for war damages).

The economies of many European countries had been seriously damaged by the Great War. The victors were deeply in debt to the United States for war loans and the defeated countries found it difficult to pay for war damages to the victors. Many soldiers came home from World War I to find no work or jobs. The Great Depression which began in the United States in 1929 was felt worldwide. Europe's economic recovery was halted. The people suffered from mass unemployment, poverty, and despair.

Nationalism was a chief cause of World War I and it grew even stronger after the war. Many Germans felt humiliated after their country's defeat in World War I and the harsh treatment under the peace treaties that their government had signed. They wished to see their country strong and powerful again. The people viewed foreigners and minority groups as inferior beings. During the 1930s, many Germans supported a violent nationalistic organization called the "Nazi Party". Nationalism was also growing in strength in Italy and Japan.

The political unrest and poor economic conditions in European countries after World War II contributed to the rise of dictatorships in several countries. During the 1920s and 1930s, dictatorships came to power in the Soviet Union (Russia), Italy, Germany and Japan. These dictators held total power and ruled without any regard for rules or laws. They used terror and secret police to crush any opposition to their rule. Those who objected or resisted were imprisoned or executed.

Remembrance Day

Information Card 5

World War II : 1939 - 1945 Cont'd

In the Soviet Union (Russia), *Joseph Stalin* became dictator in 1929. *Benito Mussolini,* leader of the Fascists, became dictator of Italy in 1922 when he and his group forced the king of Italy from his throne. Mussolini soon became known as *il Duce* (the Leader). In 1933, *Adolf Hitler*, the leader of the Nazis, was appointed chancellor of Germany. Hitler became known as *der Führer* (the leader) and soon made Germany a dictatorship. He vowed to ignore the Treaty of Versailles and promised to avenge Germany's defeat in World War I. Adolph Hitler wanted to have what he thought was a "*superior race*" and he preached that Jews and Slavs were *inferior people.* He lead a campaign of hatred against the Jews and Communists, and promised the German people to rid the country of them.

In the 1930s, military officers began to hold office in Japan's government. Its military government glorified war and the training of warriors. In 1941, *General Hideki Tojo* became premier of Japan.

Japan, Italy, and Germany invaded weak lands to expand their territories. In 1936, Germany and Italy agreed to support one another's foreign policies and formed the *Rome-Berlin Axis.* In 1940, Japan joined the alliance and it was then called the *Rome-Berlin-Tokyo Axis.* Japan's forces seized control of *Manchuria,* a region of China rich in mineral resources. In 1937, Japan launched a major attack against China. Italy looked to *Africa* to fulfill its needs and ambitions for an empire. In 1936, Ethiopia was invaded by Italian troops. The use of machine guns, tanks, and airplanes soon overpowered Ethiopia's poorly equipped army. In Germany, Hitler was building up his armed forces in violation of the Treaty of Versailles. In March 1938, German troops marched into *Austria* and united it with Germany. On September 1, 1939, Germany invaded *Poland* and began World War II. The Polish army was no match for Germany's new method of warfare called "*blitzkrieg*" or lightening war. The blitzkrieg stressed speed and surprise. Rows of tanks smashed through Poland's defences. They were able to travel deep into Poland before the Polish army had time to react. German bombers and fighter aircraft knocked out communications and pounded battle lines.

On September 3, 1939, two days after the invasion of Poland, Britain and France declared war on Germany.

Remembrance Day

Information Card 5

Important Dates to Remember

Year - 1939

September 1 - Germany invaded Poland, starting World War II.

September 3 - Britain and France declared war on Germany.

Year - 1940

April 9 - Germany invaded Denmark and Norway.

May 10 - Germany invaded Belgium and the Netherlands.

June 10 - Italy declared war on France and Great Britain.

June 22 - France signed an armistice with Germany.

July 10 - Battle of Britain began.

Year - 1941

April 6 - Germany invaded Greece and Yugoslavia.

June 22 - Germany invaded the Soviet Union (Russia).

September 8 - German troops completed the blockade of Leningrad, which lasted until January 1944.

December 7 - Japan bombed U.S. military base at Pearl Harbor in Hawaii.

December 8 - The United States, Great Britain and Canada declared war on Japan.

Year - 1942

February 15 - Singapore fell to the Japanese.

February 26 - 28 - Japan defeated an Allied naval force in the Battle of the Java Sea.

April 9 - U.S. and Philippine troops on the Bataan Peninsula surrendered.

April 18 - U.S. bombers hit Tokyo in the Doolittle raid.

May 4 - 6 - The Allies checked a Japanese assault in the Battle of the Coral Sea.

June 4 - 6 - The Allies defeated Japan in the Battle of Midway.

August 7 - U.S. marines landed on Guadalcanal.

August 25 - Hitler ordered his forces to capture Stalingrad.

Remembrance Day

Information Card 5

Improtant Dates to Remember Cont'd

October 23 - Britain attacked the Axis at El Alamein in Egypt.

November 8 - Allied troops landed in Algeria and Morocco.

Year - 1943

February 2 - The last Germans surrendered at Stalingrad.

May 13 - Axis forces in Northern Africa surrendered.

July 4 - Germany opened an assault near the Soviet city of Kursk.

July 10 - Allied forces invaded Sicily.

September 3 - Italy secretly surrendered to the Allies.

September 9 - Allied troops landed at Salerno, Italy.

November 20 - U.S. Forces invaded Tarawa.

Year - 1944

June 6 - Allied troops landed in Normandy in the D-Day invasion of northern France.

June 19 - 20 - A U.S. naval force defeated the Japanese in the Battle of the Philippine Sea.

July 10 - Allied forces invaded Sicily.

July 18 - Japan's Prime Minister Tojo resigns.

September 9 - Allied troops landed at Salerno, Italy.

October 20 - The Allies began landing in the Philippines.

October 23 - 26 - The Allies defeated Japan's navy in the Battle of Leyte Gulf in the Philippines.

December 16 - The Germans struck back at U.S. troops in the Battle of the Bulge.

Year - 1945

March 16 - U.S. marines captured Iwo Jima.

April 30 - Hitler took his life in Berlin.

May 7 - Germany surrendered unconditionally to the Allies in Reims, France ending World War II in Europe.

Remembrance Day

Information Card 5

Important Dates to Remember Cont'd

June 21 - Allied forces captured Okinawa.

August 6 - An atomic bomb was dropped on Hiroshima.

August 8 - The Soviet Union declared war on Japan.

August 9 - An atomic bomb was dropped on Nagasaki.

August 14 - Japan agreed to surrender unconditionally.

September 2 - Japan signed surrender terms aboard the battleship U.S.S. Missouri in Tokyo Bay.

The Allies

The **Allies** were countries that fought against the countries that were conquering other countries for their own purposes.

The following countries were Allies:

Argentina, Australia, Belgium, Bolivia, Brazil, Canada, Chile, China, Costa Rica, Cuba, Czechoslavakia, Denmark, Dominion Republic, Ecuador, Egypt, El Salvador, Ethiopia, France, Great Britain, Greece, Guatemala, Haiti, Honduras, India, Iran, Iraq, Lebanon, Liberia, Luxembourg, Mexico, Mongolians People's Republic, Netherlands, New Zealand, Nicaragua, Norway, Panama, Paraguay, Peru, Poland, San Marino, Saudi Arabia, South Africa, Soviet Union (Russia), Syria, Turkey, United States, Uruguay, Venezuela, Yugoslavia

The Axis

The *Axis* was the alliance of countries who were aggressively trying to take over countries to satisfy their own needs.

The following countries belonged to the Axis:

Albania, Bulgaria, Finland, Germany, Hungary, Italy, Japan, Romania, Thailand

Remembrance Day

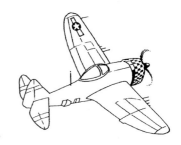

Reading Activity 5

Read the Information Cards entitled *"World War II: 1938 - 1945"*.

Carefully **read** the statements below and **classify** them as **True** or **False**.
Record the correct word on the line at the end of each statement.

1. Germany, Italy and Japan were ruled by aggressive leaders who wanted to conquer new territories to expand their countries to support their growing populations. _____

2. World War II did not have the same effect or impact on the world as World War I. _____

3. World War I had left only the defeated countries deeply in debt. _____

4. After World War I, the European countries found it difficult rebuilding their countries and their countries' economies at the same time. _____

5. Hideki Tojo, Adolph Hitler and Benito Mussolini were ambitious dictators who resented the way their countries had been treated after World War I. _____

6. Benito Mussolini, dictator of Italy, wanted a "superior race" of people and he felt that the Jews and Slavs were inferior and wanted to rid his country of them. _____

7. Japan, Italy and Germany were the Allies during World War II. _____

8. Germany used a new method of warfare called "blitzkreig" when they attacked Poland. _____

9. Germany, Japan and Italy declared war on Britain and France in 1939. _____

10. The Nazi Party was a violent organization supported by many Germans during World War II. _____

11. The United States became an ally when Japan bombed Pearl Harbor in Hawaii in 1941. _____

12. The British dropped an atomic bomb on Hiroshima and Nagasaki in Japan in 1945. _____

Remembrance Day

Information Card 6

Consequences of World War II

World War II was a very destructive war. More lives were lost in this war than in any other one. Approximately seventeen million military people who served in the armed forces for the Allies and the Axis were killed. The Soviet Union (Russia) lost more people than any other country.

Many cities lay in ruins by the end of the war especially in Germany and Japan. Aerial bombing wrecked houses, factories, and transportation and communication systems. Millions of starving and homeless people wandered through the ruined cities and land of Europe and Asia. Many civilians died during the war due to fires, diseases, and lack of health care. In the Soviet Union (Russia), 19 million Soviet civilians died and in China, ten million died due to famine.

More than twelve million people who had been uprooted from their homes and country remained in Europe after the war. These people were called *displaced persons*. They were orphans, prisoners of war, survivors of Nazi concentration camps or slave labour camps, and people who had fled invading armies and war-torn areas. Many had fled from countries in eastern Europe and refused to return to homelands that had come under communist rule.

Germany and Japan ended the war in complete defeat. Britain and France were severely weakened. The United States and the Soviet Union (Russia) emerged from the war as the world's leading powers. The Soviet Union wanted to spread *Communism* in Europe and Asia after the war to which the United States disagreed. This silence between the Soviet Union and the United States became known as the *Cold War*.

The Soviet Union came out of the war much stronger than ever before. It had also absorbed the nations of *Estonia, Latvia* and *Lithuania* before the war ended and had taken parts of *Poland, Romania, Finland* and *Czechoslovakia* by 1945. In time an "*iron curtain*" divided eastern Europe from western Europe. Behind this invisible curtain, the Soviet Union helped Communistic governments take power in Bulgaria, Czechoslovakia, Hungary, Poland, Romania, and Korea.

The *atomic bomb* opened up the *nuclear* age and a race was on to develop nuclear weapons. Since then people have feared their use.

The birth of the United Nations came out of the horror of World War II. This international organization agreed to work to promote peace. In April 1945, 50 nations gathered in San Francisco, California to draft and sign a charter for the United Nations.

Remembrance Day

Reading Activity 6

Read the Information Card entitled *"Consequences of World War II"*.

Answer each question with the correct fact/facts found on the Information Card.
Write your answers in a few words.

1. How many military people were killed in World War II? _____

2. Which country lost the most people during the war? _____

3. Why were cities lying in ruins in Germany and Japan? _____
   _____

4. What were orphans, prisoners of war, survivors of Nazi concentration camps
   called? _____

5. In what condition were Germany and Japan left at the end of the War?
   _____

6. Which two countries became the world's leading powers?
   _____

7. What type of government grew stronger after World War II? _____

8. What eventually divided Eastern and Western Europe? _____

9. What military weapon used in World War II opened up the nuclear age and
   the race for nuclear weapons? _____

10. What peace organization developed after World War II? _____
    _____

11. What was the Cold War? _____
    _____

12. In what state were many of the Europeans left when the war ended?
    _____

Remembrance Day

Information Card 7

The National War Memorial

The National War Memorial is located in Confederation Square in the city of Ottawa, Canada's capital city. This monument represents dignity, pride, courage, friendship and devotion to duty. It was erected to honour the 600 000 Canadian men and women who served and died for their country during World War I, but months after it was unveiled in 1939, World War II had begun. Today it commemorates the 1.7 million wartime soldiers who have given their lives defending our country and its freedom.

Two carved figures which represent *Peace* and *Freedom* are situated above the large stone archway of the memorial. During the day, these figures appear triumphant and free against the bright, blue sky but in the dark of the night, they look remote and aloof and appear to suggest that *Peace* and *Freedom* are not to be taken lightly. All Canadians must work hard to attain these worthy gifts.

In the centre of the monument is a large group of 25 sculptured soldiers. Their rugged, virile forms illustrate the gallant efforts made by valiant, young Canadians during the war. The 25 soldiers are raised on a pedestal and they appear to be passing through the archway as if going forward to victory. The expression on the faces of the soldiers and the way they are grouped suggests unity of purpose and a feeling of close comradeship.

The National War Memorial

Remembrance Day

Reading Activity 7

Read the information Card entitled *"The National War Memorial"*.

Locate the meanings to the following words in the dictionary. **Record** each meaning on the line beside each word.

1. dignity: _____
   _____

2. pride: _____
   _____

3. courage: _____
   _____

4. friendship: _____
   _____

5. devotion: _____
   _____

6. unveiled: _____
   _____

7. commemorates: _____
   _____

8. gallant: _____
   _____

9. valiant: _____
   _____

10. virile: _____
    _____

Remembrance Day

Information Card 8

The Remembrance Day Service At the War Memorial

World War I came to an end at 11 o'clock on November 11, 1918 -- the eleventh hour of the eleventh day of the eleventh month. The temporary peace document that was signed at the end of the war was called an armistice, which comes from Latin words that mean "*arms (or weapons) stand still*".

For many years in Canada, *Remembrance Day* was known as *Armistice Day*. In 1933 the Canadian Parliament changed the name of the holiday to Remembrance Day and made November 11 a legal holiday. After World War II, the day became a memorial day for those who died in both wars. There are still some veterans of World War II who march in Remembrance Day parades, but there are very few people alive now who took part in World War I.

On November 11, in churches, in places of work, in schools or at war memorials, people all over the world attend services of remembrance for those who died or for those who fought in the wars.

A solemn ceremony is held in Ottawa, at the National War Memorial in Confederation Square, to remember those who gave their lives for their country. Canadians from coast to coast are able to participate in this service through radio and television. The service is held in the morning. Veterans and representatives of the armed services parade around the base of the cenotaph. Bands play and choirs sing hymns of praise and thanksgiving. When the clock in the Peace Tower strikes eleven o'clock, it is a signal for the bugler to play the Last Post and the standard bearers to dip their Colors to the sound of the measured notes.

A single gun shot begins the two-minute silence. The two-minute silence is ended by the bugler calling Reveille. The Colors are raised, the bands play and the wreaths are placed at the cenotaph. The ceremony is ended with the bands playing and the spectators singing the National Anthem.

Remembrance Day

Reading Activity 8

Read the Information Card entitled *"The Remembrance Day Service at the War Memorial"*.

Complete the following activities.

a) It is November the eleventh and you are one of the spectators at the National War Memorial.

Imagine the scene that you might see

Illustrate that scene in the box below.

b) Think of the feelings that may be aroused in the participants and spectators during the ceremony.

List the words that describe the feelings of the people during the ceremony.

_____

_____

_____

_____

_____

_____

_____

_____

Remembrance Day

Information Card 9

The Two Minute Silence

During any Remembrance Day Service, the most moving and significant experience is the time when we pause, bow our heads and remember those who made the supreme sacrifice in their fight against tyranny and oppression in order to safeguard the freedom and dignity of man. During these brief two minutes, be it at a service of remembrance in a school, in a church, in a factory, in an office, or at a cenotaph, we pay homage to the courage and devotion of the brave men and women who gave their lives in the service of their country. During this moment of reflection, the busy world is quiet, the noise of the traffic diminishes, the pace of the busy city slackens, and the voices of civilized men are still.

This period of silence resulted from a recommendation made after World War I by a South African statesman, Sir James Fitzpatrick. He is possibly better known to readers as the author of the adventure book entitled "Jock of the Bushveld". As a young man, Sir James spent some years in the exciting, adventurous, and pioneer atmosphere of the gold-mining Witwatersrand. His later life was spent in the quieter setting of his South African farm. Fitzpatrick was a great lover of the wide open countryside and he spent a great deal of his time on the vast, stretching plains of his native land. The natural silence, away from the world of man, was conducive to thought and reflection. Here the past again lived in the present. Here he was inspired to make the plea that one of the finest tributes one could pay to the memory of one's comrades was to stand in silence and give one's thoughts to those who had lost their lives so that the free world might be a better place in which to live.

Remembrance Day

Reading Activity 9

Read the Information Card entitled *"The Two Minute Silence"*.

The following words were used in the story. **Match** each word in the box to its meaning. Check the dictionary if you are not sure.

sacrifice	tyranny	oppression	freedom	dignity	homage	courage
devotion	tribute	reflection	remembrance	cenotaph	civilized	

1. _____ - to give up something for the sake of something else

2. _____ - absolute power unjustly administered

3. _____ - a speech, compliment, or gift given in acknowledgement of admiration, gratitude or respect

4. _____ - respect or honour given or shown

5. _____ - the use of unjust force or authority on people

6. _____ - the state of being excellent, worthy or honorable

7. _____ - free from bondage or slavery

8. _____ - bravery, fearlessness

9. _____ - strong attachment or affection to a person or cause

10. _____ - careful thinking about something

11. _____ - showing culture, and good manners, refined, no longer savage

12. _____ - a monument erected in the memory of people buried elsewhere

Remembrance Day

Information Card 10

The Flowers of Remembrance

On Remembrance Day, everyone wears a *poppy* as a reminder of the blood-red flower that grew on the battlefields of France and Belgium where so many Canadians gave up their lives. During World War I much of the fighting was done in a place called Flanders. Every spring, the soldiers in the trenches noticed that poppies grew over the graves of their friends who were killed.

When the war ended and the soldiers came home, they still remembered their comrades who were buried in *Flanders*. When they thought of the graves, they remembered the poppies that grew around the graves. The men who returned from the war decided they would wear a poppy each year to show that they still remembered their friends.

In 1918 on November 11, the First World War ended. The men who had been in the war picked that day of each year to wear a poppy. Even people who had not been involved in the war, but who had loved the soldiers who did not return, also wore a poppy to show that they remembered the dead.

Wreaths made of poppies entwined with oak and maple leaves are placed on war memorials all across Canada on November 11 every year. A wreath is placed on the National War Memorial in Ottawa by a woman who has been chosen to represent all mothers of sons or daughters who have given their life during military service.

Real poppies were hard to obtain and there were not enough to go around. Men who had been badly wounded during World War I, and who could not work at other jobs, began to make poppies out of cloth. The early poppies were red cloth petals with black centres. This cloth poppy symbolized the real flower which grew over the graves of the men who died during World War I.

For many years after the war, children stood in silence with their parents on Remembrance Day. They all wore a poppy, stood quietly and remembered the men who had been killed during the war. When these same children grew up, there was another war. The boys who were then young men went to fight in World War II. Many of these young men were sent to the same places as the men they had stood silently for and remembered. Many of these young men died in the same places.

Remembrance Day

Information Card 10

The Flowers of Remembrance Cont'd

When World War II ended more people than ever wanted to wear a poppy. There were more men than ever to remember and honour. There were sailors and airmen as well as soldiers. These men died to protect the people who lived in Canada and those who would be born in the future.

The men who fought and died in the war wanted us to enjoy all the good things in life. They wanted our homes to be safe; they wanted us to have the opportunity to go to the school and the church of our choice.

On Remembrance Day, when everyone wears a poppy and stands in silence, we are saying "*thank you*" to all those who died for us and our country.

Remembrance Day

Reading Activity 10

Read the Information Card entitled *"The Flowers of Remembrance"*.

Answer each question with a complete sentence.

1. Why is the flower called the poppy worn on Remembrance Day?

   _____

   _____

   _____

2. After which war was the poppy chosen as the symbol of Remembrance Day?

   _____

   _____

3. Why was November 11 chosen as the day to celebrate Remembrance Day?

   _____

   _____

4. Describe the way the first poppies looked.

   _____

   _____

5. Describe the way the poppies look today.

   _____

   _____

6. Who made the first cloth poppies and why?

   _____

   _____

7. How do the mothers of lost sons and daughters pay tribute on Remembrance Day in Ottawa.

   _____

   _____

6. How do you think the women who is chosen to represent all the mothers across Canada feels that day?

   _____

   _____

Remembrance Day

Information Card 11

The Peace Tower

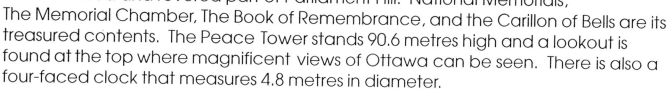

The *Peace Tower* was built to honour the sacrifices of 66 657 Canadian soldiers who laid down their lives in the cause of peace during World War I. It is the focal point of Parliament Hill and is known as one of the finest Gothic structures in the world. It is perhaps the most admired and revered part of Parliament Hill. National Memorials, The Memorial Chamber, The Book of Remembrance, and the Carillon of Bells are its treasured contents. The Peace Tower stands 90.6 metres high and a lookout is found at the top where magnificent views of Ottawa can be seen. There is also a four-faced clock that measures 4.8 metres in diameter.

The *Carillon of Bells* consists of 53 bells of varying sizes. The largest bell weighs 10 080 kilogrammes. The smallest bell weighs 4.5 kilogrammes. The beautiful instrument is played from a wooden keyboard fashioned after the 300 year old Flemish system. Musicians have come from all over the world to study the magnificently tuned Carillon.

The *Memorial Chamber* was dedicated as a memorial to Canadians who were in the First World War. It was officially opened November 11th, 1928 by Rt. Honourable William Lyon Mackenzie King, then Prime Minister. The walls and ceilings are made of a special stone that was a gift from the people of France. The border of black marble and the altar steps came from the people of Belgium. The floor is comprised of stone gathered from the various areas in which Canadian soldiers served. Inlaid brass plates denote the principal battles Canadians fought in such as Ypres, Mount Sorrel, Somme, Vimy Ridge, Hill 70, Passchendaele, Amiens, Arras, Cambrai, Valenciennes, Mons.

The walls of the Memorial Chamber hold carved marble panels that tell the Canadian story during the war to end all wars. Each panel illustrates the sacrifices and achievements of the Canadian Armed Forces during 1914 to 1918 of World War I.

Within the Memorial Chamber is found the Altar of Sacrifice. It holds the Book of Remembrance in a gold frame decorated with the Royal Arms and the Arms of Canada. The name of each Canadian soldier who gave his life in the service of his country appears in the Book. The pages are turned according to a calendar so that each is on view the same day of the same month in each year.

The Books of Remembrance of World War II, the Korean War, South African War and the Nile Expedition are also found within the Memorial Chamber.

Remembrance Day

Reading Activity 11

Read the Information Card entitled "The Peace Tower".

Answer each question with a complete sentence answer.

1. What is the Peace Tower?

_____

_____

2. Why is it famous?

_____

_____

3. What are the four treasured contents stored in the Peace Tower?

_____

_____

_____

_____

4. How many bells are found in the Carillon?

_____

_____

5. What is the special room in the Peace Tower called?

_____

_____

6. List the things that you would see in the Memorial Chamber.

_____

_____

_____

_____

_____

7. What would you find in the Books of Remembrance?

_____

_____

8. Why do you think it is important to remember the men that died during wars?

_____

_____

_____

Remembrance Day

Information Card 12

Famous Canadian War Heroes

During the First and Second World Wars many men and women fought and many died defending Canada. Many of our young Canadian men performed heroic and daring deeds in the throes of battle. Read about the adventures of some of our famous Canadian War Heroes.

Billy Barker

Billy Barker was born in 1894 in Dauphin, Manitoba. He was one of the greatest fighter pilots of World War I. Billy Barker shot down 53 enemy aircraft during the war. He was known for the different methods that he used while shooting down the enemy. His tactics were quite different than other pilots. Billy flew a plane called a Sopwith Camel. This type of plane was quite agile at low altitudes and manoeuvred well in a limited air space.

Billy would lure the enemy down to his level by flying close to the ground instead of diving on his enemy from above. His ability to manoeuvre his Sopwith Camel easily at low altitudes was an advantage over the faster German planes.

During the war, Billy Barker and his squadron attacked many airbases in northern Italy and they virtually grounded the Austrian Air Force. In the last month of the war, he performed his most outstanding feat. On a flight to England, all by himself, he took on 60 enemy aircraft. He succeeded in downing five of the enemy aircraft before he went crashing to the ground. He amazingly survived the crash and was awarded the Victoria Cross for his incredible air battle.

In 1930, after the war, Billy Barker died when the airplane he was flying crashed at Rockcliffe Air Station in Ottawa.

Buzz Beurling

Buzz Beurling was born in 1921 in Verdun, Québec. He was one of the most outstanding pilots during World War II. At the age of fourteen he flew his first plane, and at seventeen he won an aerobatic competition. Unfortunately, due to not enough education, he could not join the Royal Canadian Air Force.

Remembrance Day

Information Card 12

Famous Canadian War Heroes Cont'd

Buzz wanted to participate in the war effort and applied to the Royal Air Force in Britain. He was accepted by Britain and became one of their star pilots. In 1942, he played an important part in the successful defence of the island of Malta. While helping to defend Malta from the German and Italian forces, he shot down 27 enemy aircraft in less than five months.

Buzz transferred to the Royal Canadian Air Force because he had achieved fame for his efforts defending Malta. Unfortunately, he was not happy in the Canadian Air Force. Buzz was very much a loner, and was better at making decisions than at taking orders. He resigned from the Royal Canadian Air Force in 1944.

Four years later, he decided to help Israel fight its war against the Arabs. Unfortunately he died on the way to Israel when his plane caught fire over an airfield outside of Rome, Italy.

Billy Bishop

Billy Bishop was born in Owen Sound, Ontario in 1894. He was one of the most famous air aces of World War I. He became famous for his phenomenal record of having shot down 72 enemy planes.

Billy often went out alone and would fly far behind enemy lines. He would make surprise attacks on German air bases. His type of courage was considered the most difficult kind, "the courage of the early morning". He was awarded the Victoria Cross as well as other medals for his bravery and incredible feats.

After the war, Billy married Timothy Eaton's granddaughter and he became a successful businessman. For a while, he ran a small aviation business with his partner Billy Barker who was also a war hero. Later, he became an oil executive. During the Second World War, he was an honourary Air Marshal, in charge of recruiting young people into the air force. He helped boost the war effort.

Remembrance Day

Information Card 12

Famous Canadian War Heroes Cont'd

A. Roy Brown

A. Roy Brown was born in Carleton Place, Ontario in 1893. He was a fighter pilot during World War I. During the war, he was the famous pilot who shot down Germany's greatest air ace, the famous *Red Baron, Manfred von Richthofen.*

On the day this exciting event took place, a young inexperienced Canadian pilot named Wop May was on his first combat fight. The famous Red Baron was right behind Wop May pursuing him. A. Roy Brown saw what was going to happen and began firing at the Red Baron's plane. At the same time, the Australian gunners were firing from the ground. They also hit the Red Baron's plane and just who was responsible for shooting down the Red Baron's plane was disputed for a long time. A. Roy Brown was certain he had, but it now seems likely that it was an Australian bullet that actually killed the Red Baron.

During the war A. Roy Brown was suffering from battle fatigue and actually fainted while flying his plane causing it to crash. He pulled through and survived the crash even though he was not expected to live. After the war he went into his own air service business.

Andrew Mynarski

Pilot Officer Andrew Mynarski was born in Winnipeg, Manitoba in 1916. He is considered the most heroic of all the Canadian war heroes. One day while on a mission his plane was attacked and eventually caught on fire. He ordered all of his crew to bail out of the blazing aircraft. Unfortunately the rear gunner couldn't as he was trapped in his turret. Mynarski fought through the flames and tried to free the gunner. It was a fruitless effort and the gunner insisted that he at least save himself. Mynarski went back through the flames to the escape hatch.

As a last effort to encourage the trapped gunner, Mynarski stood at attention and saluted the gunner even though his parachute and clothes were on fire. Then he jumped to safety. Mynarski was very badly burned and later died of his injuries. The gunner surprisingly survived the crash, and lived to tell of the pilot's amazing courage. In 1944 Mynarski was awarded a posthumous Victoria Cross.

Remembrance Day

Reading Activity 12

Read the Information Cards entitled *"Famous Canadian War Heroes"*.

Read each statement carefully. Which Canadian War Hero is the statement describing?

Record the name of the War Hero on the line in the statement.

Billy Bishop	Buzz Beurling	Billy Barker	A. Roy Brown	Andrew Mynarski

1. _____ claimed he shot down the famous German war ace, Manfred von Richthofen.

2. _____ lost his life trying to save a trapped gunner on his burning plane.

3. _____ could not join the Royal Canadian Air Force because he didn't have the required education.

4. _____ had a phenomenal record of shooting down 72 enemy planes.

5. _____ shot down 53 enemy aircraft during World War I.

6. _____ suffering from battle fatigue, fainted during a flight causing his plane to crash.

7. _____ 's type of courage was known as "the courage of early morning".

8. _____ died of his injuries while his trapped gunner lived to tell about his heroic deed.

9. _____ and _____ became business partners after the First World War.

10. _____ flew a plane called the Sopwith Camel.

11. _____ flew his first plane at the age of fourteen.

12. _____ became famous while defending the island of Malta during the Second World War.

Remembrance Day

Information Card 13

John McCrae

John McCrae was born in Guelph, Ontario in 1872. He was the younger of two brothers. His father, Captain David McCrae who commanded the Ontario Field Battery, owned a woollen mill in Guelph.

John attended the University of Guelph and became a doctor. During his university days, he liked to write poetry and several of his poems were published in magazines and newspapers.

In 1899, he enlisted as a lieutenant in the Canadian Field Artillery for duty in the South African War or Boer War. When the war ended, he returned to being a doctor and to writing poetry.

When World I began, he joined the First Canadian Contingent. He became a major and First Brigade Artillery surgeon and was stationed in Flanders during the spring of 1915. His medical station was located on the banks of the Ypres Canal near the village of Ypres.

On May 2, 1915, one of John McCrae's close friends, Alexis Helmer, was killed during the Second Battle of Ypres. The next morning one of his friends, Sergeant-Major Allinson, saw him sitting on the step of an ambulance writing on a pad of paper. Sergeant-Major Allinson noticed that his face was calm but tired and that his eyes frequently strayed to Helmer's grave. The poem that he wrote was an exact description of the scene in front of him. Larks were really flying overhead, while artillery boomed at the front and poppies fluttered in the breeze between the crosses. The poem that he had written was called "In Flanders Fields". This poem made John McCrae famous throughout the world.

John McCrae was killed by the war but not by a bullet or shell. The time that he had spent fighting in the Boer War in Africa and in the First World War broke down his health until he died of pneumonia and meningitis on January 28, 1918.

His uniforms and personal effects went down in a ship that was torpedoed. However many of his letters, newspaper clippings and other memorabilia are found at his home in Guelph. John McCrae's home is now open to the public as a tourist attraction.

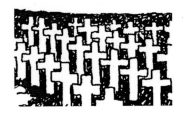

Remembrance Day

Reading Activity 13

Read the Information Card entitled *"John McCrae"*.

Search for a copy of his poem "In Flanders Fields" in a poetry book.

Carefully read the poem imagining the scene that John McCrae saw while he wrote it.

Copy the poem in your best handwriting.

Illustrate the scene that you think John McCrae saw while he sat writing his poem.

_____

_____

_____

_____

_____

_____

_____

_____

_____

_____

Remembrance Day

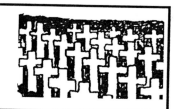

Word Study Activity 1

Lest We Forget Crossword Puzzle

Complete the Remembrance Day crossword puzzle.

Carefully read the puzzle clues.

Remembrance Day

Lest We Forget Crossword Puzzle Clues

Across

2. a large piece of war equipment used on land
4. the name of the city where the first atomic bomb was dropped
5. a cemetery for dead soldiers
11. the leader of England during World War II
13. a time when we bow our heads and remember those who died during the wars
14. an American port bombed by the Japanese during World War Two
16. the name of the day of the large invasion on the beaches of Normandy
17. It is placed on a cenotaph.
18. Japanese pilots who crashed their planes deliberately on ships
19. a blood-red flower
20. the name of a famous Remembrance Day poem

Down

1. They marked the graves of dead soldiers.
3. a famous German leader
6. a song played during a Remembrance Day Service by a bugler
7. the name of the day World War I ended
8. another name for monument
9. the author of "In Flanders Fields"
10. the name of a German war attack
12. a famous Canadian flyer during World War I
15. Manfred von Richthofen's nickname

Answers

In Flanders Fields	Armistice Day	John McCrae	D-Day
Hiroshima	Sherman Tank	Billy Bishop	wreath
Two-Minute Silence	Winston Churchill	Red Baron	Last Post
Pearl Harbor	Adolph Hitler	kamikaze	blitzkreig
Flanders Fields	cenotaph	poppy	crosses

Remembrance Day

Word Study Activity 2

Remembrance Day Word Search

Circle all the words in the word search that pertain to Remembrance Day.

There are **20** words. Can you find them all?

I found _____ words.

```
J  O  H  N  M  C  C  R  A  E  X  V  X  X  C  C  M
I  S  I  L  E  N  C  E  I  I  H  E  H  H  N  N  N
L  L  D  N  N  O  S  P  N  M  R  T  X  V  N  U  I
V  F  V  U  T  T  T  O  V  V  V  E  X  X  Y  Y  Y
Y  L  Y  Y  T  E  E  E  L  B  K  R  P  P  P  V  V
E  A  E  H  H  Y  H  N  N  D  A  A  U  U  P  A  C
J  N  J  J  L  L  W  D  Q  Q  I  N  A  A  O  D  R
D  D  N  N  Q  Q  R  C  D  E  E  E  D  B  P  B  O
H  E  M  U  U  E  E  R  A  R  X  R  S  P  H  S  S
O  R  O  U  N  U  A  N  P  R  Y  B  B  B  Y  O  S
O  S  N  I  O  R  T  O  R  Y  E  Y  Y  D  D  N  E
O  F  U  I  V  D  H  T  T  T  T  M  Y  Y  Y  O  S
I  I  M  I  E  E  O  A  D  D  D  Z  E  Z  U  U  U
I  E  E  O  M  A  O  P  B  B  B  X  X  M  U  R  U
O  L  N  Z  B  D  Q  H  Q  Q  O  O  O  B  B  B  W
C  D  T  C  E  D  D  D  N  N  P  R  A  I  S  E  A
N  S  N  N  R  N  S  E  D  A  R  A  P  N  N  N  R
```

Look for these words:

silence	parades	remember	cenotaph
honour	duty	crosses	wreath
soldier	John McCrae	D-Day	November
war	Flanders Fields	poppy	praise
dead	monument	bands	veteran

Remembrance Day

Word Study Activity 3

Syllabication

The words below are the names of countries and cities that were involved in both World Wars.

Rewrite each name on the line provided dividing it into syllables.

Example: England - Eng / land

1. Normandy _____
2. Dunkirk _____
3. Japan _____
4. Italy _____
5. Nagasaki _____
6. Belgium _____
7. Holland _____
8. Germany _____
9. Berlin _____
10. London _____
11. Paris _____
12. Switzerland _____
13. Poland _____
14. Russia _____
15. Moscow _____
16. China _____
17. Australia _____
18. Canada _____
19. Denmark _____

Remembrance Day

Word Study Activity 4

Matching Antonyms

The words "**win**" and "**lose**" have the opposite meanings.

Words with opposite meanings are called **antonyms**.

Beside each word **print** its antonym from the list in the box on the line.

1. war _____

2. remember _____

3. bravery _____

4. courage _____

5. victory _____

6. fight _____

7. build _____

8. silent _____

9. proud _____

10. alive _____

11. freedom _____

12. friend _____

dead
ashamed
slavery
enemy
surrender
defeat
cowardice
fearful
destroy
noisy
forget
peace

Choose **two** pairs of **antonyms**. Use each pair in a good sentence that shows their true meanings.

_____

_____

_____

_____

_____

_____

_____

Remembrance Day

Word Study Activity 5

Matching Synonyms

The words "**mean**" and "**cruel**" have the same meanings.

Words that have the same or similar meanings are called **synonyms**.

Choose a word from the box to match each word below. **Write** the word on the line provided.

1. friends	_____	sacrifice
2. ditch	_____	responsibility
3. monument	_____	comrades
4. honour	_____	assasin
5. brave	_____	winners
6. glory	_____	trench
7. duty	_____	cenotaph
8. praise	_____	remember
9. courage	_____	fearless
10. devotion	_____	fame
11. terror	_____	loyalty
12. killer	_____	oppression
13. victors	_____	fear
14. tyranny	_____	valour
15. to give up something	_____	laud

 # Remembrance Day

Word Study Activity 6

Writing the Plural Form

The word "**airplanes**" is a plural word.

A plural word means more than one. **Example**: body - bodies

Sometimes the ending of the root word must change when you make the singular word plural. **Watch** the ending of each word.

Beside each word below **record** its plural form on the line.

1. enemy   _____
2. poppy   _____
3. cross   _____
4. army   _____
5. memory   _____
6. torpedo   _____
7. trench   _____
8. bomb   _____
9. spy   _____
10. veteran   _____
11. duty   _____
12. warship   _____
13. soldier   _____
14. cenotaph _____
15. hero   _____
16. ally   _____
17. wreathe   _____
18. ceremony _____

 # Remembrance Day

Word Study Activity 7

Working with Parts of Speech

Nouns, verbs, adjectives and *adverbs* are parts of speech found in sentences.
Classify the words in the list on the chart under the correct heading.

Nouns	Verbs
_____	_____
_____	_____
_____	_____
_____	_____

Adjectives	Adverbs
_____	_____
_____	_____
_____	_____
_____	_____

soldier

fight

proudly

valiant

bravely

blood-red

poppy

bombed

remember

cenotaph

daring

silently

gallant

wreath

march

peacefully

Remembrance Day

Word Study Activity 8

Spelling Riddles

The answer to each clue is hidden in the words

Remembrance Day

Use only the number of letters that are in the words.

1. an animal's home _____ _____ _____

2. a month _____ _____ _____

3. a place to sleep _____ _____ _____

4. a colour _____ _____ _____

5. a another name for taxi _____ _____ _____

6. to run in one _____ _____ _____ _____

7. a nickname for a famous war pilot _____ _____ _____

8. an animal that has a shell _____ _____ _____ _____

9. to have a great deal _____ _____ _____ _____

10. a large farm building _____ _____ _____

11. very thick milk _____ _____ _____ _____

12. to mend holes in socks _____ _____ _____ _____

13. belongs to a club _____ _____ _____ _____ _____

14. the opposite to women _____ _____ _____

15. to move to music _____ _____ _____ _____ _____

16. something that happens when you sleep _____ _____ _____ _____ _____

17. close by _____ _____ _____ _____

18. to be cruel _____ _____ _____ _____

19. made from flour _____ _____ _____ _____ _____

20. a large group of musicians _____ _____ _____ _____

Remembrance Day

Word Study Activity 9

Anagrams

Take a word that you have heard before.

Add a letter to it.

A Remembrance Day world will soon appear.

It's easy. Try to do it.

Remember that you will have to **rearrange** the letters in the words too.

1. sank   + t   = _____ _____ _____ _____
2. mob   + b   = _____ _____ _____
3. lean   + p   = _____ _____ _____ _____ _____
4. van   + y   = _____ _____ _____ _____
5. wheat + r   = _____ _____ _____ _____ _____ _____
6. drape + a   = _____ _____ _____ _____ _____ _____
7. harm   + c   = _____ _____ _____ _____ _____
8. sand   + b   = _____ _____ _____ _____ _____
9. cape   + e   = _____ _____ _____ _____ _____
10. toil   + p   = _____ _____ _____ _____ _____
11. gift   + h   = _____ _____ _____ _____ _____
12. bleat + t   = _____ _____ _____ _____ _____ _____
13. ram   + y   = _____ _____ _____ _____
14. roots + p   = _____ _____ _____ _____ _____ _____
15. sun   + g   = _____ _____ _____ _____
16. tough + f   = _____ _____ _____ _____ _____ _____
17. drip   + e   = _____ _____ _____ _____ _____
18. rise   + n   = _____ _____ _____ _____ _____
19. down   + u   = _____ _____ _____ _____ _____
20. bear   + v   = _____ _____ _____ _____ _____

Remembrance Day

Creative Writing Activity 1

Poetry Search

Search through poetry books and find a poem about Remembrance Day.

Read the poem carefully.

Copy the poem in your **best** handwriting.

Illustrate the poem that you chose in detail.

Display them on a piece of construction paper.

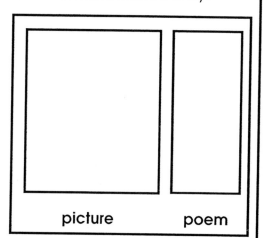

picture   poem

Remembrance Day

Creative Writing Activity 2

A Sentence of Remembrance

It is important to remember people who have sacrificed their lives to keep our country free and safe.

Create your own sentence of remembrance for Remembrance Day.

Example:

Let us remember the men and women who laid down their lives for their country and died in a far away places.

_____

_____

_____

_____

_____

_____

Remembrance Day

Creative Writing Activity 3

Sentences of Thanksgiving

On Remembrance Day there are many things for which we show our thanks.

Create your own sentences of thanksgiving for Remembrance Day

Example:

Let us be thankful for all the blessings that we enjoy in this great land.

Write **three** good sentences of thanksgiving.

_____

_____

_____

_____

_____

Remembrance Day

Creative Writing Activity 4

Remembrance Day Thoughts

Write a paragraph on your thoughts and feelings about Remembrance Day.

Example:

Remembrance Day is a symbol that reminds us of empty houses and children who grew up without parents. We remember the unfortunate men who lost an arm or leg in the line of duty and were crippled for life. Remembrance Day reminds us to always be on the alert for anything that might threaten our freedom.

_____

_____

_____

_____

_____

_____

Remembrance Day

Creative Writing Activity 5

Story Writing

Write a descriptive, exciting story using one of the following titles or make up one or your own.

1. An Act of Courage
2. Being a War Hero
3. Killed in Action
4. Fighting in the Trenches
5. Why Wear a Poppy?
6. Billy Bishop, Flying Ace
7. The Day I Remembered......

8. Our Escape Through the Mountains
9. The Day the War Ended
10. Remembrance Day Sights and Sounds
11. Hiding From the Germans
12. I'll never forget..............
13. No more War
14. Peace at Last

Remembrance Day

Creative Writing Activity 6

A Remembrance Day Card

Design a Remembrance Day card that you might send to a mother who has lost a son or daughter or husband during one of the wars or during a peace keeping mission today.

Illustrate the front of the card in a creative way or make your card in the shape of a symbol pertaining to Remembrance Day.

Write meaningful thoughts on the inside of the card.

Example:

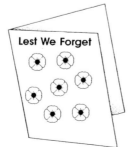

Lest We Forget

Remembrance Day

Creative Writing Activity 7

Writing a Stair Poem

A stair poem is one in which the ideals build up like stairs.

Step One - name of a person or thing

Step Two - three describing words or action words

Step Three - a place you would find the person or thing

Step Four - another name for the person or thing

Example:

```
                                                    Warrior
                                 In the trenches
              Brave, valiant, devoted
Soldier
```

Remembrance Day

Creative Writing Activity 8

A Cinquain of Remembrance

A cinquain is a simple, five line poem. Each line has a special number of syllables.

_____

_____

_____

_____

_____

2 syllables - **title**

4 syllables - **description of the title**

6 syllables - **action words**

8 syllables - **how you feel about the title**

2 syllables - **another name for the title**

Example:

Pilots
Driver of planes
Swooping, diving, shooting
Men who perform dangerous feats
Flyers

Write your own cinquain poem and **illustrate** it.

Remembrance Day

Creative Writing Activity 8

Remembrance Day Haiku

A *haiku* is a Japanese poem which is only three lines long.

Each line has a special number of syllables.

Line One - _____ five syllables
Line Two - _____ seven syllables
Line Three - _____ five syllables

Example:
Growing in Flanders
Between the stark, white crosses
Bright, blood-red poppies

Write your own Remembrance Day haiku and **illustrate** it.

Remembrance Day

Creative Writing Activity 9

Acrostic Poetry

An *acrostic poem* is one where each letter of a word is used as the first letter for one line of the poem.

Example:
W ars are deadly
A rmies fighting fiercely
R uining cities and towns
S oldiers dying in the battlefields

Choose a word that pertains to peace, to war, or to Remembrance Day.

Make up your own acrostic poem about it.

Illustrate your acrostic poem.

Remembrance Day

Brainstorming Activity 1

If you could wish upon a star.......

What **three** Remembrance Day wishes would you make for your country and the people living in the world today?

Write your three wishes in complete sentences.

Star the wish that you feel is the most important.

Tell why you feel that the wish that you starred is the most important.

Remembrance Day

Brainstorming Activity 2

Remembrance Day is ....

Remembrance Day has many meanings for different people in the world.

In a paragraph or two, express your feelings about Remembrance Day.

Use the sentence below as a beginning.

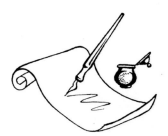

"To me the most important things about Remembrance Day are........................

Remembrance Day

Brainstorming Activity 3

War Alert!

There have been many explosive, angry confrontations taking place in several countries throughout the world.

The leader of your country makes an sudden press conference on television.

He announces that there might be another world war.

This upsets you a great deal so you decide to **write** a letter to the Prime Minister of Canada.

In your letter, express your feelings and concerns about his announcement.

Remembrance Day

Brainstorming Activity 4

A Remembrance Day Poster

We should never forget the many Canadian men and women who sacrificed their lives so we might live in peace.

Design a poster to advertise Remembrance Day.

On your poster **illustrate** a meaningful picture or symbols that relate to Remembrance Day.

Neatly **print** a meaningful saying and the date on it.

Display your poster in the school to remind the students of the approaching day.

Remembrance Day

Brainstorming Activity 5

Fighting at the Front

Imagine being a soldier in World War I or World War II fighting from a trench or on a foreign battlefield.

Think of the feelings that you might have, the sounds that you might hear and the sights that you might see.

Make a chart like the one below.

On the chart **record** your feelings and observations

Feelings	Sounds	Sights

Remembrance Day

Brainstorming Activity 6

Acts of Courage

During the wars many soldiers, sailors and pilots displayed great acts of courage or bravery.

Some even risked their lives while performing their duty .

It is just not military people who show acts of courage or bravery. Often, ordinary citizens have risked their lives to save people or animals.

Think of times, places or events when anyone would have to show courage or bravery.

Make a list of these courageous deeds.

Remembrance Day

Brainstorming Activity 7

Planning an Interview

Pretend that you are going to interview a veteran from World War II or a military person presently working in one of the armed services.

Think of things that you might ask him/her during the interview.

Make a list of **ten** good questions that you might ask.

Write up your interview as a story and read it to the class.

Remembrance Day

Brainstorming Activity 8

Ruled by a Dictator

Adolph Hitler was the leader in Germany that started World War II by invading and conquering countries in order to gain more land.

He wanted to develop a superior race of people by eliminating people he did not feel were good enough.

Imagine what the world would be like today if Adolph Hitler had succeeded in winning World War II.

Write a paragraph or two describing your ideas of a world lead by a leader like Adolph Hitler.

Remembrance Day

Brainstorming Activity 9

An Honour Roll

The names of Canadian men and women who died during the two wars are written or inscribed on an Honour Roll.

Think of other Canadians who have accomplished brave or courageous deeds but were never involved in a war.

Write their names on an Honour Roll.

Beside each name **write** the brave or courageous deed each one performed.

Try to think of **five** Canadians

Example:

Terry Fox
  Attempted to run across Canada with an artificial leg in order to raise money for Cancer research

---

Remembrance Day

Research Activity 1

War Leaders

Choose **one** of the famous war leaders below.

Adolph Hitler

Franklin D. Roosevelt

Winston Churchill

Joseph Stalin

Benito Mussolini

Hideki Tojo

Find out **ten** interesting facts about the leader that you chose.

Record the facts in complete sentences to form two paragraphs.

Famous Canadian Honour Roll

Name	Deed
1. _____	_____
	_____
	_____
2. _____	_____
	_____
	_____
3. _____	_____
	_____
	_____
4. _____	_____
	_____
	_____
5. _____	_____
	_____
	_____

Remembrance Day

Research Activity 2

The Flower of Remembrance

Poppies grew over the graves of soldiers who died in Flanders Fields during World War I.

The poppy has been a symbol of Remembrance Day for many years.

Look in the encyclopedia and find out **five** interesting facts about the real poppy.

Write the facts in complete sentences.

Illustrate the poppy.

Remembrance Day

Research Activity 3

Important Places

There were many places during the wars that became famous due to an important event happening there.

Using the encyclopedias or reference books, try to find out the importance of each place during the wars.

Flanders Fields

Hiroshima

Dunkirk

Pearl Harbor

Normandy

Remembrance Day

Research Activity 4

Researching a Country

There were many countries involved in World War II.

Listed below are the names of some of them.

Germany   *Great Britain*
France   *The Netherlands*
Italy   *Japan*
United States   *Poland*
Russia   *Canada*
Australia   *Austria*

Choose the country that interests you.

Find out **ten** interesting facts about the country.

Remembrance Day

Research Activity 5

Canadian Medals

Many Canadians were presented with medals during the two wars for outstanding deeds.

The *Victoria Cross* is one of the most important medals given.

Research and find out why it is important and what it looks like.

Illustrate and **label** other medals that you find interesting.

Remembrance Day

Research Activity 6

War Machines

During the wars many different types of equipment were used.

Look through some reference books to find different war machines.

Illustrate and **label** six different types.

Complete this assignment as a chart.

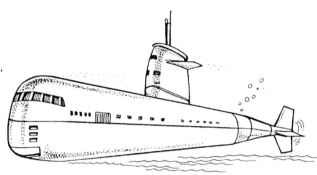

Remembrance Day

Research Activity 7

The Atomic Bomb

The Atomic Bomb was dropped on Hiroshima and Nagasaki, two cities in Japan, during World War II, in order to end the war.

Research to find out the effects that the blast from an Atomic Bomb has.

Express your feelings on the use of Nuclear Arms by countries in the world today.

Remembrance Day

Research Activity 8

Fun With Maps

Use an atlas to locate the names of the countries and cities below that were involved in the Second World War.

Score a point for every place that you are able to locate on a map.

You have **fifteen** minutes to work on the activity.

Starting Time: _____   Stopping Time: _____

Countries

1. Argentina _____
2. Australia _____
3. Venezuela _____
4. Belgium _____
5. Boliva _____
6. Canada _____
7. Chile _____
8. China _____
9. Columbia _____
10. Cuba _____
11. Czechoslavkia _____
12. Denmark _____
13. Egypt

14. France _____
15. Brazil _____
16. Great Britain _____
17. Greece _____
18. India _____
19. Mexico _____
20. New Zealand _____
21. Peru _____
22. Poland _____
23. Russia _____
24. Turkey _____
25. Norway _____

Cities

1. Berlin _____
2. London _____
3. Tokyo _____
4. Hiroshima _____
5. Nagasaki _____

6. Pearl Harbour _____
7. Warsaw _____
8. Rome _____
9. Paris _____

Count your points carefully.

My score is _____ points.

Lest We Forget

Answer Key

Reading Activity 1: *(page 14)*
1. • People wanted more land to grow food.
   • Some wars were caused for greed and the want of money.
   • Governments caused wars to increase their power and unite the people.
   • Countries feared being attacked by other nations and attacked them first.
   • Sometimes countries disagree over certain things.
   • Religious beliefs often caused wars.
2. Reasons are the answers given to the people by the government for the war in order to unite them. The reasons are usually lofty and noble. The causes of a war may be for selfish, base, or wicked ideals.
3. People hate wars because they bring hardship and suffering.
4. Answers will vary.

Reading Activity 2: *(page 18)*
1. The assasination of Archduke Francis Ferdinand and his wife of Austria-Hungary in Sarajevo.
2. **a)** It was the site of many small wars.
   b) There are still wars and fighting going on in this area. Example Serajevo, Bosnia
3. Canada belonged to the British Commonwealth and was loyal to Britain.
4. There were 32 100 troops.
5. It was the first time gas was used.
6. It was the battle of Vimy Ridge.
7. Billy Bishop was awarded the Victoria Cross.
8. **a)** Conscription means the compulsory enlistment of men into the military.
   b) Answers will vary.
9. Roy Brown was credited with shooting down the Red Baron.
10. It ended on November 11, 1918.

Reading Activity 3: *(page 21)*
1. Germany, England, battleships, seapower
2. Tanks, barbed, trenches
3. machine, gun's, slaughtered
4. soldiers, trenches
5. no man's land, difficult
6. miserable, wet, uncomfortable
7. artillery, machine, guns
8. gas, vomiting, suffocation
9. enemy
10. airplane, combat
11. Technology, industrialization, destructive
12. France, Belgium, Germany

Reading Activity 4: *(page 23)*
1. Many important buildings, churches and - Paragraph #2
2. Factories, bridges and railroad tracks - Paragraph #2

3. Nearly ten million soldiers died - Paragraph #1
4. Millions of people were uprooted - Paragraph #6
5. When the war was over - Paragraph #3
6. Four monarchies toppled after the - Paragraph #4
7. Russia and Germany gave up - Paragraph #5
8. Many people chose to make - Paragraph #6
9. They did not want to - Paragraph #6
10. European attitudes and ideals had - Paragraph #6
11. Finland and the Baltic States - Paragraph #5
12. Soldiers returning home did not - Paragraph #3

Reading Activity 5: *(page 29)*
1. True   2. False   3. False   4. True   5. True   6. False   7. False
8. True   9. False   10. True   11. True   12. False   13. False   14. True

Reading Activity 6: *(page)*
1. 17 million
2. Soviet Union
3. aerial bombing wrecked them
4. displaced persons
5. in complete defeat
6. Soviet Union and the United States
7. communism
8. an "iron curtain"
9. the atomic bomb
10. The United Nations
11. silence between the Soviet Union and the United States   12. homeless and starving

Reading Activity 7: *(page 33)*
1. *dignity*: the quality of character or ability that wins respect and high opinion of others
2. *pride*: a high opinion of one's own worth or possessions, something a person is proud of
3. *courage*: bravery, meeting courage without fear, fearlessness
4. *friendship*: the condition of being friends, a liking between friends
5. *devotion*: deep, steady affecton, loyalty, faithfulness
6. *unveiled*: to remove a veil from, to uncover a statue or a monument
7. *commemorates*: to honour the memory of, observe, celebrate
8. *gallant*: noble in spirit and in conduct, valiant, brave, high spirited, heroic
9. *valiant*: having courage, brave, courageous
10. *virile*: manly, masculine

Reading Activity 8: *(page 35)*
Answers will vary.

Reading Activity 9: *(page 37)*
1. sacrifice   2. tyranny   3. tribute   4. homage   5. oppression   6. dignity
7. freedom   8. courage   9. devotion   10. reflection   11. civilized   12. cenotaph

Reading Activity 10: *(page 40)*
1. It is a reminder of the blood-red flower that grew on the battlefields of France and Belgium and over the graves of men who gave up their lives.
2. It was chosen after World War I.
3. World War I ended on November 11.
4. The first poppies had red cloth petals with a black centre.

5. Today's poppies are red plastic covered with a fuzzy material with a black centre.
6. Men who had been badly injured during World War One and who could not work at other jobs made the poppies by hand out of red cloth.
7. One mother is picked to place the wreath on the monument for all the other mothers.
8. Answers will vary.

Reading Activity 11: *(page 42)*
1. a monument   2. finest Gothic structure in the world   3. National Memorials, The Memorial Chamber, The Book of Remembrance, The Carillon of Bells
4. 53 bells   5. The Memorial Chamber   6. stone walls, black marble, brass plates carved marble panels, the Altar of Sacrifice, Books of Remembrance
7. name of Canadian soldiers who died in the wars   8. Answers will vary.

Reading Activity 12: *(page 46)*
1. A. Roy Brown   2. Andrew Mynarski   3. Buzz Beurling   4. Billy Bishop
5. Billy Barker   6. A. Roy Brown   7. Billy Bishop   8. Andrew Mynarski
9. Billy Bishop, Billy Barker   10. Billy Barker   11. Buzz Beurling
12. Buzz Beurling

Reading Activity 13: *(page 48)*
Answers will vary.

Word Study Activity 1: *(page 49)*   **Lest We Forget Crossword Puzzle**

Word Study Activity 2: (page 51)   Remembrance Day Word Search

```
J  O  H  N  M  C  C  R  A  E  X  V  X  X  C  C  M
I  S  I  L  E  N  C  E  I  I  H  E  H  H  N  N  N
L  L  D  N  N  O  S  P  N  M  R  T  X  V  N  U  I
V  F  V  U  T  T  T  O  V  V  V  E  X  X  X  Y  Y
Y  L  Y  Y  T  E  E  E  L  B  K  R  P  P  P  V  V
E  A  E  H  H  Y  H  N  N  D  A  A  U  U  P  A  C
J  N  J  J  L  L  W  D  Q  Q  I  N  A  A  O  D  R
D  D  N  N  Q  Q  R  C  D  E  E  E  D  B  P  B  O
H  E  M  U  U  U  E  E  R  A  R  X  R  S  P  H  S
O  R  O  U  N  U  A  N  P  R  Y  B  B  B  Y  O  S
O  S  N  I  O  R  T  O  R  Y  E  Y  Y  D  D  N  E
O  F  U  I  V  D  H  T  T  T  M  Y  Y  Y  O  O  S
I  I  M  I  E  E  O  A  D  D  D  Z  E  Z  U  U  U
I  E  E  O  M  A  O  P  B  B  B  X  X  M  U  R  U
O  L  N  Z  B  D  Q  H  Q  Q  O  O  O  B  B  B  W
C  D  T  C  E  D  D  D  N  N  P  R  A  I  S  E  A
N  S  N  N  R  N  S  E  D  A  R  A  P  N  N  N  R
```

Word Study Activity 3: (page 52)

1. Nor-man-dy
2. Dun-kirk
3. Ja-pan
4. I-ta-ly
5. Na-ga-sa-ki
6. Bel-gium
7. Hol-land
8. Ger-man-y
9. Ber-lin
10. Lon-don
11. Pa-ris
12. Swit-zer-land
13. Po-land
14. Rus-sia
15. Mos-cow
16. Chi-na
17. Aus-tra-li-a
18. Can-a-da
19. Den-mark

Word Study Activity 4: (page 53)

1. peace
2. forget
3. cowardice
4. fearful
5. defeat
6. surrender
7. destroy
8. noisy
9. ashamed
10. dead
11. slavery
12. enemy

Word Study Activity 5: (page 54)

1. comrades
2. trench
3. cenotaph
4. remember
5. fearless
6. fame
7. responsibility
8. laud
9. valour
10. loyalty
11. fear
12. assasin
13. winners
14. oppression
15. sacrifice

Word Study Activity 6: (page 55)

1. enemies
2. poppies
3. crosses
4. armies
5. memories
6. torpodoes
7. trenches
8. bombs
9. spies
10. veterans
11. duties
12. warships
13. soldiers
14. cenotaphs
15. heroes
16. allies
17. wreaths
18. ceremonies

Word Study Activity 7: *(page 56)*

Nouns: soldier, poppy, cenotaph, wreath
Verbs: fight, bombed, remember, march
Adjectives: valiant, blood-red, daring, gallant
Adverbs: proudly, bravely, silently, peacefully

Word Study Activity 8: *(page 57)*

1. den	2. May	3. bed	4. red	5. cab	6. race
7. ace	8. crab	9. many	10. barn	11. cream	12. darn
13. member	14. men	15. dance	16. dream	17. near	18. mean
19. bread	20. band				

Word Study Activity 9: *(page 58)*

1. tanks	2. bomb	3. plane	4. navy	5. wreath	6. parade
7. march	8. bands	9. peace	10. pilot	11. fight	12. battle
13. army	14. troops	15. guns	16. fought	17. pride	18. siren
19. wound	20. brave				

S & S Snip Art for Remembrance Day

79